# NURTURING THE PRESENT

## Unlocking the Power of Mindfulness to Transform Your Life and Well-Being

**RICHARD FRANCIS**

# Table of contents

# INTRODUCTION

In our fast-paced, constantly connected world, it's easy to become overwhelmed by the demands of daily life. We often find ourselves caught up in regrets about the past or anxieties about the future, leaving little room for truly experiencing the present moment. Yet, it is precisely in the present where we find the key to a more fulfilling and balanced life. "Nurturing the Present: Unlocking the Power of Mindfulness to Transform Your Life and Well-Being" is designed to guide you on a journey to reclaim the present moment, using mindfulness as a powerful tool for transformation.

Mindfulness, at its core, is about paying deliberate attention to the present moment with a sense of openness and non-judgment. It encourages us to fully engage with our current experiences, rather than being lost in thoughts of what was or what might be. This practice is rooted in ancient traditions, yet its principles are universally applicable and profoundly relevant in our modern lives. By fostering a mindful approach, we can cultivate a deeper sense of awareness, clarity, and peace, transforming how we relate to ourselves and the world around us.

The essence of mindfulness lies in its simplicity. It's about being fully present in each moment, embracing our experiences without distraction or distortion. However, achieving this state of presence can be challenging, especially with the constant barrage of information and demands we face daily. This book aims to demystify mindfulness and offer practical, actionable strategies to help you integrate it into your life seamlessly.

In Chapter 1, we delve into the concept of mindfulness, exploring its origins and the substantial scientific evidence supporting its benefits. Understanding the historical and research-backed foundations of mindfulness provides a solid basis for appreciating its potential impact on our well-being.

Chapter 2 focuses on the present moment, highlighting its significance and the common barriers that prevent us from fully engaging with it. We will examine how our minds often wander and the techniques that can help anchor us in the here and now. By learning to recognize and overcome these barriers, we can enhance our ability to live more fully in each moment.

Developing a mindfulness practice is the focus of Chapter 3. We will introduce simple exercises designed for beginners, offering guidance on creating a daily mindfulness routine. This chapter also explores how mindfulness can be incorporated into everyday activities, making it an accessible and practical tool for enhancing daily life.

Despite the many benefits of mindfulness, there are challenges that can arise. Chapter 4 addresses these challenges, such as dealing with distractions, managing stress, and overcoming negative thought patterns. By providing strategies to navigate these obstacles, this chapter aims to empower you to maintain and deepen your mindfulness practice.

Emotional well-being is a central theme in Chapter 5. Mindfulness can profoundly impact how we understand and manage our emotions, fostering greater compassion, self-acceptance, and healthier relationships. This chapter explores how mindfulness can be a powerful tool for emotional growth and interpersonal harmony.

In Chapter 6, we shift our focus to personal growth. Mindfulness can play a crucial role in setting meaningful goals, embracing change, and unlocking our creative potential. This chapter offers insights into how mindfulness can support your journey toward a more balanced and fulfilling life.

Integrating mindfulness into daily life is the focus of Chapter 7. Whether it's mindful eating, working, or engaging with others, this chapter provides practical advice on how to weave mindfulness into various aspects of your routine. We'll explore how mindfulness can enhance problem-solving and decision-making, contributing to a more harmonious and effective approach to life.

For those who wish to explore mindfulness at a deeper level, Chapter 8 introduces advanced practices and techniques. This chapter covers meditation practices, ways to deepen your mindfulness journey, and how to integrate mindfulness with other wellness practices. It also provides resources for finding communities and furthering your practice.

The conclusion reflects on the journey through the book, emphasizing the importance of continuing your mindfulness practice and integrating its principles into your life. It serves as a reminder that mindfulness is an ongoing process, one that evolves with time and practice.

"Nurturing the Present" is more than a guide to mindfulness; it is an invitation to live more fully and authentically in the present moment. By unlocking the power of mindfulness, you can transform your life and well-being, finding peace and fulfillment in the here and now. Join me on this journey, and let's embrace the present together.

# CHAPTER 1

# UNDERSTANDING MINDFULNESS

Mindfulness is more than just a buzzword or a fleeting trend; it is an ancient practice that has withstood the test of time, offering profound benefits to those who embrace it. At its core, mindfulness is the practice of bringing one's attention to the present moment with an attitude of openness, curiosity, and non-judgment. It is about being fully aware of what is happening both inside and outside of us, without becoming entangled in our thoughts, emotions, or surroundings. In this chapter, we will explore the origins of mindfulness, its evolution over the centuries, and the compelling scientific evidence that supports its effectiveness in enhancing our mental, emotional, and physical well-being.

## The Origins and Evolution of Mindfulness

The roots of mindfulness can be traced back to ancient Eastern spiritual traditions, particularly within Buddhism, where it was regarded as a fundamental aspect of the path to enlightenment. The practice was known as "sati" in Pali, a term that encompasses awareness, attention, and remembering. In Buddhist teachings, mindfulness is one of the Noble Eightfold Path's key elements, essential for cultivating wisdom and ethical conduct. However, the concept of mindfulness is not exclusive to Buddhism. Similar practices can be found in other spiritual traditions, such as Hinduism, Taoism, and even early Christian contemplative practices.

Over the centuries, mindfulness remained largely within the confines of religious and spiritual contexts. It wasn't until the 20th century that mindfulness began to be explored outside these frameworks, largely due to the efforts of pioneers like Jon Kabat-Zinn, who introduced Mindfulness-Based Stress Reduction (MBSR) in the 1970s. Kabat-Zinn's work marked a significant turning point, bringing mindfulness into the realm of modern medicine and psychology. His program was designed to help people manage chronic pain and stress through mindfulness practices, and it quickly gained recognition for its effectiveness.

This secularization and adaptation of mindfulness made it accessible to a broader audience, leading to its widespread adoption in various fields, including healthcare, education, business, and even sports. Today, mindfulness is practiced by millions worldwide, not as a religious or spiritual exercise, but as a practical tool for enhancing overall well-being.

## The Core Principles of Mindfulness

At the heart of mindfulness lies a few core principles that guide its practice. The first is intentionality—the deliberate act of paying attention to the present moment. This involves consciously directing our awareness to what is happening right now, rather than allowing our minds to drift to past regrets or future worries. This principle helps us cultivate a deeper connection with our current experiences.

Another fundamental principle is non-judgment. In mindfulness practice, we observe our thoughts, feelings, and sensations without labeling them as good or bad, right or wrong. This attitude of acceptance allows us to experience things as they are, without the added layer of interpretation or judgment that often distorts our perception. By embracing non-judgment, we learn to be kinder to ourselves and others, fostering a sense of compassion and understanding.

Curiosity and openness are also central to mindfulness. Rather than approaching our experiences with preconceived notions or expectations, mindfulness encourages us to be curious about what unfolds in the present moment. This open-mindedness allows us to discover new perspectives and insights that we might otherwise overlook. It also helps us remain flexible and adaptable in the face of life's challenges.

## The Science Behind Mindfulness

In recent decades, the practice of mindfulness has gained significant attention from the scientific community. Numerous studies have explored its effects on the brain, body, and overall well-being, leading to a growing body of evidence that supports its benefits.

One of the most well-documented effects of mindfulness is its ability to reduce stress. Research has shown that mindfulness practices can lower levels of cortisol, the hormone associated with stress, thereby helping individuals manage anxiety and tension more effectively. This stress-reducing effect is particularly beneficial in today's fast-paced world, where chronic stress is a common issue.

Mindfulness has also been shown to enhance emotional regulation. By bringing awareness to our emotions without judgment, we can observe them without becoming overwhelmed. This practice allows us to respond to our emotions more skillfully, rather than reacting impulsively. Studies have found that mindfulness can increase activity in the prefrontal cortex, the part of the brain responsible for executive functions such as decision-making and emotional regulation, while decreasing activity in the amygdala, which is associated with fear and anxiety.

Cognitive benefits are another area where mindfulness has shown promise. Regular mindfulness meditation has been shown to increase attention, concentration, and memory. It enhances our ability to focus on tasks and maintain attention, which is crucial for both personal and professional success. Moreover, mindfulness can help break the cycle of rumination—repetitive negative thinking that often contributes to depression and anxiety.

Beyond mental and emotional well-being, mindfulness has been associated with physical health benefits as well. For instance, it has been found to improve immune function, lower blood pressure, and reduce symptoms of chronic pain. These physical benefits are thought to result from mindfulness's ability to promote relaxation and reduce the physiological effects of stress.

## The Essence of Mindfulness

Mindfulness, in its simplest form, is the practice of being fully aware and present in the moment. It is about paying close attention to our thoughts, feelings, and sensations without becoming caught up in them or allowing them to dominate our actions. This practice encourages us to observe our experiences with clarity and openness, rather than reacting to them automatically or impulsively.

At its core, mindfulness is about presence—being here, right now, without distraction. It is the ability to tune into the current moment with all of our attention and awareness, letting go of distractions from the past or anxieties about the future. By anchoring ourselves in the present, we cultivate a sense of calm and clarity that can profoundly impact our overall well-being.

The essence of mindfulness lies in the quality of attention we bring to our experiences. This attention is characterized by non-judgment, meaning we observe what is happening without labeling it as good or bad, desirable or undesirable. Instead of trying to change or resist what we are experiencing, we simply allow it to unfold, accepting it as it is. This non-judgmental stance helps us cultivate a deeper sense of acceptance and peace, as we learn to let go of the need to control every aspect of our lives.

Curiosity is another essential aspect of mindfulness. Approaching our experiences with a sense of curiosity means being open to whatever arises, without preconceived notions or expectations. It involves seeing things as if for the first time, with fresh eyes and an inquisitive mind. This attitude of curiosity allows us to discover new insights and perspectives, helping us break free from habitual patterns of thinking and behaving.

Compassion also plays a crucial role in mindfulness. When we practice mindfulness, we develop a compassionate attitude towards ourselves and others. This compassion arises from the non-judgmental and curious attention we bring to our experiences. By acknowledging our thoughts and emotions without criticism or harshness, we create a space for self-compassion and understanding. This, in turn, fosters greater empathy and kindness towards others, as we recognize the shared human experience of struggle and growth.

Mindfulness is not about escaping from life's challenges or seeking a state of perpetual calm. Instead, it is about fully engaging with life as it is, with all its ups and downs. It teaches us to be present with whatever is happening, whether it is pleasant or unpleasant, joyful or painful. By doing so, we develop the resilience to navigate life's difficulties with greater ease and grace.

One of the most powerful aspects of mindfulness is its ability to connect us with our true selves. In the hustle and bustle of daily life, it is easy to lose sight of who we are and what truly matters to us. Mindfulness helps us reconnect with our inner values, desires, and aspirations. By paying attention to the present moment, we gain clarity about our thoughts, feelings, and motivations, allowing us to make choices that align with our authentic selves.

# CHAPTER 2

# THE PRESENT MOMENT

The present moment is the only point in time that we truly have. It is where life unfolds, yet it is often the most overlooked and undervalued aspect of our existence. Many of us spend a significant portion of our lives caught up in thoughts about the past or worries about the future, neglecting the richness of the present. In this chapter, we will explore the significance of the present moment, why it is so challenging to remain fully present, and how we can begin to cultivate a deeper connection to it.

## The Significance of the Present Moment

The present moment is where our lives actually happen. While the past is a collection of memories and the future is a projection of our hopes or fears, the present moment is real and immediate. It is the only time when we can truly experience life—whether through the sensation of the wind on our skin, the sound of a loved one's voice, or the taste of a meal. By grounding ourselves in the present, we allow ourselves to fully engage with the world around us, fostering a deeper sense of connection and awareness.

Living in the present moment also has profound implications for our mental and emotional well-being. When we focus on the here and now, we are less likely to get lost in regret over past events or anxiety about future possibilities. This shift in focus can reduce stress and improve our overall quality of life. Moreover, being present allows us to respond to life's challenges more effectively, as we are not clouded by distractions or reactive emotions. In this way, the present moment becomes a powerful tool for navigating the complexities of life with greater clarity and calm.

## Why We Struggle to Stay Present

Despite the benefits of being present, many of us find it difficult to maintain a steady connection to the present moment. This difficulty often stems from the nature of the mind itself. Our minds are naturally inclined to wander, constantly jumping between thoughts of the past and the future. This tendency is known as "time-traveling," where our thoughts drift into memories or fantasies, taking us away from the immediate experience of the present.

One reason for this mental time-traveling is our inherent desire to avoid discomfort. The present moment can sometimes be uncomfortable or challenging, and our minds may try to escape this discomfort by dwelling on past pleasures or imagining future successes. However, this avoidance only serves to deepen our disconnection from the present, leaving us feeling unfulfilled and anxious.

Another factor that contributes to our struggle to stay present is the modern world's constant barrage of distractions. With the ubiquity of smartphones, social media, and instant communication, it is easier than ever to become absorbed in activities that pull us away from the present. These distractions fragment our attention, making it difficult to fully engage with the moment at hand.

## Techniques to Cultivate Presence

Cultivating a deeper connection to the present moment requires intentional practice. The following techniques can help you develop this skill, allowing you to experience the richness of each moment more fully.

**1. Mindful Breathing:** One of the simplest ways to anchor yourself in the present moment is through mindful breathing. By focusing on the sensation of your breath as it enters and leaves your body, you create a natural point of focus that draws your attention away from distracting thoughts. This practice can be done anywhere, at any time, and serves as a powerful tool for returning to the present.

**2. Sensory Awareness:** Engaging your senses is another effective way to connect with the present. Take a moment to notice the sounds around you, the textures you can feel, the colors you can see, or the smells and tastes you can detect. By fully immersing yourself in these sensory experiences, you become more attuned to the present moment and less likely to be swept away by your thoughts.

**3. Grounding Exercises:** Grounding exercises are designed to bring your attention back to the present moment by focusing on your physical connection to the world around you. For example, you might place your feet firmly on the ground and feel the support of the earth beneath you, or you might hold an object and focus on its texture and weight. These exercises help create a sense of stability and presence, especially during moments of stress or anxiety.

**4. Observing Your Thoughts:** Another key aspect of cultivating presence is learning to observe your thoughts without getting caught up in them. When a thought arises, try to notice it without judgment or attachment. Imagine that your thoughts are like clouds passing through the sky—acknowledge them, but let them drift by without pulling you away from the present. This practice can help you develop a more detached relationship with your thoughts, making it easier to stay grounded in the here and now.

**5. Mindful Listening:** Engaging in mindful listening can also enhance your connection to the present moment. When someone is speaking to you, give them your full attention without planning your response or letting your mind wander. Truly listen to their words, the tone of their voice, and the emotions they are expressing. This practice not only strengthens your relationships but also deepens your presence in the moment.

**6. Daily Rituals:** Incorporating mindfulness into your daily routines can help reinforce your connection to the present moment. Whether it's drinking your morning coffee, taking a walk, or brushing your teeth, treat these activities as opportunities to practice mindfulness. Pay attention to each action, savoring the experience without rushing through it or allowing your mind to drift.

## Common Barriers to Being Present

Despite the benefits of living in the present moment, many of us find it challenging to stay fully engaged with the here and now. Several barriers can prevent us from being present, often leading to a sense of disconnection from our lives and a heightened experience of stress or dissatisfaction. Understanding these barriers is the first step toward overcoming them and cultivating a deeper sense of mindfulness.

### 1. Mind-Wandering

One of the most significant barriers to being present is mind-wandering. The human mind has a natural tendency to drift away from the current moment, often without us even realizing it. Our thoughts can easily shift to past experiences, future plans, or daydreams, pulling us away from what is happening right now. While some degree of mind-wandering is normal and can even be beneficial for creativity and problem-solving, excessive mind-wandering can lead to a lack of focus and a diminished ability to engage with the present moment. This mental distraction often leaves us feeling scattered and disconnected, unable to fully appreciate our current experiences.

## 2. Attachment to the Past

Another common barrier to being present is our attachment to the past. Many people find themselves ruminating over past events, whether it's regrets about things they wish they had done differently or nostalgia for times when life seemed better. This preoccupation with the past can trap us in a cycle of negative thinking, preventing us from fully engaging with the present. By continually replaying past events in our minds, we miss out on the opportunities and experiences available to us right now.

## 3. Anxiety About the Future

Just as we can become trapped by the past, anxiety about the future is another significant obstacle to being present. Worrying about what might happen, planning for every possible outcome, or fearing the unknown can consume our mental energy, making it difficult to focus on the present moment. This forward-thinking mindset, while sometimes necessary for practical purposes, can become overwhelming when it takes over our thoughts. When we are constantly focused on the future, we are unable to appreciate the present moment for what it is, leading to increased stress and a diminished sense of well-being.

## 4. Overstimulation and Distractions

In today's fast-paced world, we are constantly bombarded with stimuli and distractions that pull our attention away from the present moment. Smartphones, social media, and the demands of modern life can make it difficult to maintain a steady focus on the here and now. The constant influx of information and the pressure to multitask can fragment our attention, leading to a scattered mind and a diminished ability to be present. This overstimulation can also lead to mental fatigue, making it even harder to stay engaged with the current moment.

## 5. Emotional Avoidance

Emotional avoidance is another barrier to being present. When we encounter uncomfortable emotions such as sadness, anger, or fear, our natural tendency might be to avoid or suppress these feelings rather than face them head-on. This avoidance often leads us to distract ourselves with thoughts, activities, or other forms of escape, pulling us away from the present moment. While it may seem easier to avoid difficult emotions, this approach ultimately prevents us from fully experiencing and processing our feelings, leading to a sense of disconnection from ourselves and the present.

## 6. Perfectionism

Perfectionism can also hinder our ability to be present. When we are constantly striving for an unattainable standard, we become preoccupied with the outcomes of our actions rather than the process itself. This focus on perfection can cause us to miss out on the joys and learning opportunities that come from being fully engaged in the present moment. Instead of appreciating the journey, we become fixated on the destination, leading to frustration and a diminished sense of satisfaction.

## Overcoming Barriers to Presence

Recognizing these common barriers is the first step toward overcoming them. By becoming aware of the factors that pull us away from the present moment, we can begin to develop strategies to counteract them. This might involve practicing mindfulness techniques, such as grounding exercises or mindful breathing, to bring our attention back to the here and now. It also requires a commitment to self-compassion, allowing ourselves to be imperfect and embracing the present moment as it is, without judgment or expectation.

# CHAPTER 3
# DEVELOPING A MINDFULNESS PRACTICE

Mindfulness is more than just a concept; it is a practice that requires dedication, intention, and consistency. Developing a mindfulness practice involves learning specific techniques, creating a routine, and cultivating the right mindset. While the journey of mindfulness is deeply personal, there are universal strategies and principles that can guide anyone interested in integrating mindfulness into their daily life.

## Understanding the Importance of Regular Practice

At the heart of mindfulness is the idea of being fully present in the moment. However, achieving this state consistently requires regular practice. Just as physical exercise strengthens the body, mindfulness exercises strengthen the mind's ability to stay present and focused. The benefits of mindfulness, such as reduced stress, improved emotional regulation, and enhanced well-being, are not immediate but accumulate over time with consistent practice.

Regular practice helps to rewire the brain, making mindfulness a more natural and automatic response to life's challenges. Studies have shown that mindfulness can lead to changes in brain structure and function, particularly in areas associated with attention, emotional regulation, and self-awareness. This neuroplasticity underlines the importance of making mindfulness a daily habit rather than an occasional activity.

## Setting the Foundation: Creating a Mindful Environment

One of the first steps in developing a mindfulness practice is creating an environment that supports your practice. A mindful environment is one that is calm, quiet, and free from distractions. This space should be a sanctuary where you can retreat from the busyness of everyday life and focus inward.

Start by choosing a specific spot in your home where you will practice mindfulness regularly. This space should be comfortable, whether it's a corner of your bedroom, a dedicated meditation room, or even a quiet spot in your garden. Consider adding elements that promote calmness and focus, such as soft lighting, comfortable seating, and perhaps a few items that inspire tranquility, like candles, plants, or meaningful objects.

It's also important to set boundaries around your mindfulness space. Let those you live with know that when you are in this space, you should not be disturbed. This not only helps you maintain focus but also reinforces the importance of your practice in your daily routine.

## Establishing a Routine: Consistency is Key

Mindfulness, like any other skill, requires consistent practice. Establishing a routine is crucial for making mindfulness a regular part of your life. Begin by choosing a specific time each day for your practice. Many people find that early morning or late evening works best, as these times are often quieter and allow for a peaceful transition into or out of the day.

Start with a realistic commitment. If you're new to mindfulness, it's better to start with shorter sessions, perhaps 5 to 10 minutes, and gradually increase the time as you become more comfortable with the practice. The key is to be consistent, even if it means practicing for just a few minutes each day. Over time, these small moments of mindfulness will accumulate, leading to significant benefits.

## Core Techniques for Mindfulness Practice

There are several core techniques that form the foundation of mindfulness practice. Each technique offers a different approach to cultivating presence and awareness, and they can be practiced individually or combined depending on your needs and preferences.

### 1. Mindful Breathing

Mindful breathing is one of the simplest and most accessible forms of mindfulness practice. It entails focusing your attention on your breath and noticing the sensations of each inhalation and exhalation. The goal is not to control your breathing but to observe it with a sense of curiosity and openness.

To practice mindful breathing, find a comfortable seated position, close your eyes, and bring your attention to your breath. Notice where you feel your breath most clearly—whether it's in your nostrils, chest, or abdomen. Whenever your mind wanders, gently guide it back to the breath without judgment. Over time, this practice can help you develop a more focused and calm mind.

## 2. Body Scan Meditation

Body scan meditation involves systematically focusing on different parts of your body, bringing awareness to any sensations, tension, or discomfort that may be present. This practice helps to connect the mind with the body and is particularly effective for reducing stress and promoting relaxation.

To practice a body scan, lie down or sit comfortably and close your eyes. Begin by focusing on your toes, noticing any sensations there, and then gradually move your attention up through your body—your feet, legs, abdomen, chest, arms, hands, and head. As you focus on each area, observe any physical sensations, and if you encounter tension, try to release it with your breath.

### 3. Mindful Walking

Mindful walking is a practice that involves bringing full awareness to the act of walking. Unlike regular walking, mindful walking is done slowly and deliberately, with attention to each step and the sensations it creates.

To practice mindful walking, find a quiet place where you can walk undisturbed. Begin by standing still, feeling the ground beneath your feet. As you start to walk, focus on the movement of your feet, the shift in your balance, and the feeling of the ground with each step. Try to keep your attention on the physical experience of walking, letting go of any thoughts that arise. This practice can be particularly grounding and is a great way to integrate mindfulness into daily activities.

### 4. Loving-Kindness Meditation

Loving-kindness meditation, also known as Metta, is a practice that involves cultivating feelings of compassion and love for yourself and others. This practice can be particularly powerful for developing a more positive and empathetic outlook on life.

To practice loving-kindness meditation, find a comfortable seated position, close your eyes, and bring to mind a series of phrases such as "May I be happy, may I be healthy, may I be protected, may I live comfortably." Repeat these statements silently, first toward oneself, then toward others—beginning with loved ones, then acquaintances, and then extending them to all beings. This practice helps to foster a sense of connection and compassion, both for yourself and others.

## Overcoming Challenges in Mindfulness Practice

Developing a mindfulness practice is not without its challenges. Common obstacles include restlessness, boredom, frustration, and the inevitable wandering mind. These challenges are normal and part of the process. The key is to approach them with patience and self-compassion.

When you encounter restlessness or boredom, try to observe these feelings without judgment. Recognize that it's natural for the mind to resist stillness, especially when it's used to constant stimulation. Instead of fighting these feelings, acknowledge them, and gently bring your focus back to the practice.

If your mind keeps wandering, remember that mindfulness is about noticing when this happens and gently guiding your attention back to the present moment. Over time, you'll find that your ability to stay focused improves, but it's important to be kind to yourself during this process. The goal is not to achieve perfect focus but to cultivate a gentle awareness of the present.

# Integrating Mindfulness into Daily Life

While formal meditation practices are essential, mindfulness is ultimately about bringing awareness into every aspect of your life. This means practicing mindfulness not just during meditation but throughout your day—in your interactions with others, in your work, and even in mundane activities like eating or washing dishes.

One way to integrate mindfulness into daily life is by setting reminders to pause and take a few deep breaths throughout the day. These mini mindfulness moments can help you stay grounded and connected to the present, even amidst a busy schedule.

Another approach is to practice mindfulness during routine activities. For example, when eating, focus on the taste, texture, and aroma of your food. When talking to someone, listen fully without planning your response or letting your mind wander. These practices help to reinforce the habit of mindfulness, making it a natural part of your daily life.

## The Long-Term Benefits of a Mindfulness Practice

The long-term benefits of a consistent mindfulness practice are profound. Over time, mindfulness can lead to greater emotional resilience, improved focus and concentration, enhanced relationships, and a deeper sense of peace and well-being. As you continue to practice, you may find that mindfulness becomes not just something you do, but a way of being—a lens through which you experience the world with greater clarity, compassion, and presence.

## Tools and Resources for Mindfulness Practice

Embarking on a mindfulness journey requires more than just intention—it often helps to have the right tools and resources to support and enhance your practice. These tools can make mindfulness more accessible, provide guidance, and help sustain a consistent practice. Whether you're just beginning or looking to deepen your mindfulness routine, exploring different tools and resources can help you find what resonates best with you.

## 1. Meditation Apps

Meditation apps have become increasingly popular as convenient tools for mindfulness practice. They offer a wide range of guided meditations, breathing exercises, and mindfulness techniques that cater to various experience levels, from beginners to seasoned practitioners. Some of the most well-known apps include Headspace, Calm, Insight Timer, and Ten Percent Happier.

These apps are designed to fit into busy lifestyles, allowing you to practice mindfulness anytime, anywhere. They offer features like progress tracking, reminders, and themed courses that focus on specific areas such as stress reduction, sleep improvement, or emotional resilience. For those who prefer structure and guidance, meditation apps can be a valuable resource, making it easier to maintain a regular practice.

## 2. Books and Audiobooks

Books and audiobooks provide in-depth insights and practical advice on mindfulness, making them excellent resources for those who prefer to learn through reading or listening. There are countless books on mindfulness, ranging from introductory guides to more advanced explorations of the practice.

Some classic mindfulness books include "The Miracle of Mindfulness" by Thich Nhat Hanh, "Wherever You Go, There You Are" by Jon Kabat-Zinn, and "Radical Acceptance" by Tara Brach. These books not only explain the principles of mindfulness but also offer exercises and reflections to help readers integrate mindfulness into their daily lives. Audiobooks are a great alternative for those who prefer to listen while on the go, allowing you to absorb wisdom and techniques while commuting, walking, or relaxing at home.

### 3. Mindfulness Journals

Mindfulness journals are an excellent tool for reflecting on your practice and tracking your progress. These journals often include prompts that encourage you to write about your experiences, thoughts, and feelings during mindfulness practice. They can help you deepen your awareness, recognize patterns, and identify areas for growth.

Using a mindfulness journal can also enhance your practice by providing a space to record your daily intentions, gratitude lists, and insights gained through meditation. Over time, this reflective practice can help you see how mindfulness is impacting your life and provide motivation to continue.

### 4. Online Courses and Workshops

Online courses and workshops offer structured learning opportunities for those interested in deepening their mindfulness practice. Many organizations and mindfulness teachers offer online courses that cover various aspects of mindfulness, from beginner fundamentals to advanced practices.

Courses like Mindfulness-Based Stress Reduction (MBSR), developed by Jon Kabat-Zinn, are widely recognized for their effectiveness in teaching mindfulness skills that can reduce stress and improve overall well-being. These courses often include video lessons, guided practices, and opportunities for interaction with instructors and other participants, making them a comprehensive resource for learning mindfulness.

## 5. Mindfulness Communities

Joining a mindfulness community, whether online or in-person, can provide valuable support and encouragement. These communities offer a space to share experiences, ask questions, and connect with others who are also practicing mindfulness. Many meditation centers, yoga studios, and wellness organizations offer mindfulness groups or classes where participants can practice together and learn from each other.

Online forums and social media groups also offer opportunities to connect with like-minded individuals, share resources, and find inspiration. Being part of a community can help you stay committed to your practice, provide accountability, and offer a sense of belonging as you navigate your mindfulness journey.

## 6. Mindfulness Retreats

For those seeking an immersive experience, mindfulness retreats offer the opportunity to deepen your practice in a focused, supportive environment. Retreats can range from a weekend to several weeks and are often held in serene locations that promote relaxation and introspection.

During a retreat, participants typically engage in extended periods of meditation, mindful movement, and silence, allowing for deep self-reflection and rejuvenation. Retreats are led by experienced teachers who provide guidance and support, making them an excellent resource for those looking to make significant progress in their mindfulness practice.

# CHAPTER 4

# OVERCOMING CHALLENGES WITH MINDFULNESS

Embarking on a mindfulness journey can be profoundly transformative, offering a pathway to greater clarity, emotional resilience, and overall well-being. However, like any meaningful endeavor, mindfulness practice is not without its challenges. As with any skill, the process of developing mindfulness can be met with obstacles that may cause frustration or discouragement. Recognizing and overcoming these challenges is an essential part of the mindfulness journey, as it allows us to deepen our practice and experience its full benefits.

## The Challenge of Restlessness and Discomfort

One of the most common challenges in mindfulness practice is dealing with restlessness and discomfort. When sitting in meditation or practicing mindfulness, it's not uncommon to experience physical discomfort, such as aches, itches, or the urge to move. Similarly, mental restlessness may arise, making it difficult to stay focused and still.

To overcome physical discomfort, it's important to find a comfortable posture before beginning your practice. This might mean sitting on a cushion, using a chair with proper back support, or lying down if necessary. However, some level of discomfort is inevitable, and mindfulness practice offers an opportunity to explore our relationship with discomfort. Instead of immediately reacting to the sensation, try observing it with curiosity and acceptance. Notice how the discomfort feels, where it is located, and whether it changes over time. Often, simply acknowledging the sensation can reduce its intensity.

Mental restlessness is another common challenge. Our minds are used to constant stimulation, and when we try to slow down and focus, it can feel unnatural. When you notice your mind becoming restless, rather than getting frustrated, gently guide your attention back to the present moment. It can be helpful to anchor your awareness in your breath, a particular sensation, or the sound around you. Remember, the goal is not to suppress thoughts or sensations but to observe them without getting swept away.

## Facing Emotional Turbulence

Mindfulness practice can bring us face-to-face with difficult emotions that we might typically avoid or suppress. As we slow down and pay attention, feelings of sadness, anger, anxiety, or fear may surface. This can be unsettling, especially if we're not used to dealing with these emotions head-on.

Overcoming this challenge involves approaching emotions with the same curiosity and non-judgmental awareness that we bring to other aspects of mindfulness. Instead of trying to push away uncomfortable emotions, allow yourself to feel them fully. Recognize that emotions are transient—they arise, linger for a while, and eventually pass. By acknowledging and accepting these emotions, you allow yourself to process them healthily rather than letting them fester beneath the surface.

It can be helpful to practice self-compassion during these moments. Remind yourself that it's okay to feel what you're feeling and that everyone experiences difficult emotions from time to time. Practicing loving-kindness meditation, where you extend compassion toward yourself, can also help you navigate emotional turbulence with greater ease.

## Dealing with Boredom and Monotony

Boredom is another challenge that often arises in mindfulness practice. Repeating the same meditation or focusing on the same sensations can feel monotonous, leading to disengagement. This boredom can be particularly pronounced for those new to mindfulness, who might expect each session to be a novel or enlightening experience.

The key to overcoming boredom lies in shifting your perspective. Instead of seeing boredom as a negative experience, approach it as an opportunity to deepen your practice. Boredom often arises when we're not fully present or when we're expecting something other than what is happening right now. When boredom arises, notice it without judgment. Investigate what boredom feels like in your body and mind. Is it a restless energy? A lack of interest? A feeling of impatience?

By observing boredom mindfully, you can learn to sit with it without needing to change or escape it. This practice teaches patience and equanimity, helping you to remain engaged even when things seem mundane. Over time, you may find that what once felt boring becomes rich with subtle details and insights, as mindfulness reveals layers of experience that were previously overlooked.

## Overcoming the Wandering Mind

A wandering mind is perhaps the most common challenge faced in mindfulness practice. No matter how focused you try to be, it's inevitable that your mind will drift away from the present moment—often multiple times within a single session. This can lead to frustration, especially when you feel like you're constantly battling your thoughts.

To overcome this challenge, it's important to reframe your understanding of what mindfulness practice entails. The goal is not to stop your mind from wandering but to become aware of when it does. Each time you notice your mind has drifted, that's a moment of mindfulness. Instead of viewing it as a failure, recognize it as a success—an opportunity to bring your attention back to the present.

You can also use techniques to gently guide your mind back. Focusing on the breath is a common method, but you can also anchor your awareness to a specific sensation in your body, a sound, or even a word or phrase (a mantra). With practice, you'll notice that your mind wanders less frequently, and when it does, you'll be able to bring it back with greater ease.

## The Illusion of Progress

Mindfulness, by its nature, is a practice that often resists quantification. Unlike other pursuits where progress can be easily measured, the benefits of mindfulness may be subtle and slow to emerge. This can lead to frustration or the belief that you're not making progress, especially if you don't notice immediate changes in your mental state or well-being.

Overcoming this challenge requires patience and trust in the process. Mindfulness is not about achieving a particular state or outcome; it's about developing a relationship with the present moment, whatever it contains. Trust that even when it feels like you're not progressing, the simple act of practicing mindfulness is creating change on a deeper level.

It can be helpful to occasionally reflect on your practice. Consider how you reacted to stress or discomfort before you began mindfulness and how you respond now. You might notice subtle shifts in your emotional resilience, your ability to stay present, or your overall sense of well-being. These reflections can help you see the progress that might not be immediately apparent in day-to-day practice.

## Integrating Mindfulness into a Busy Life

One of the biggest challenges people face with mindfulness is integrating it into a busy life. With so many demands on our time, it can feel difficult to carve out space for regular mindfulness practice. This challenge is particularly pronounced in a world that values productivity and constant activity.

To overcome this challenge, it's important to shift your mindset around mindfulness. Instead of seeing it as another task on your to-do list, view mindfulness as a way to enhance the quality of everything you do. Mindfulness doesn't require hours of meditation each day; it can be practiced in small moments throughout your routine.

Consider starting with just a few minutes of mindfulness each day. You can integrate mindfulness into daily activities like eating, walking, or even brushing your teeth. These small moments of presence can accumulate, creating a more mindful approach to life overall. Over time, you may find it easier to prioritize more formal mindfulness practice, as you begin to experience the benefits in your daily life.

# Managing Stress and Anxiety through Mindfulness

In today's fast-paced world, stress and anxiety have become almost ubiquitous experiences. From demanding work schedules to personal responsibilities, many people find themselves caught in a cycle of chronic stress that can have serious implications for both mental and physical health. While stress is a natural response to life's challenges, when it becomes overwhelming, it can lead to anxiety, burnout, and a host of other health issues. Mindfulness offers a powerful and accessible way to manage stress and anxiety, helping individuals cultivate a sense of calm and balance amidst the chaos of daily life.

## The Nature of Stress and Anxiety

Stress is the body's natural response to perceived threats or challenges. When faced with a stressful situation, the body goes into "fight or flight" mode, releasing stress hormones like cortisol and adrenaline to prepare for action.

While this response can be helpful in short bursts, chronic stress keeps the body in a state of heightened alertness, which can lead to long-term health problems such as high blood pressure, digestive issues, and weakened immunity.

Anxiety, on the other hand, is often a response to stress that manifests as excessive worry or fear about future events. While occasional anxiety is a normal part of life, chronic anxiety can interfere with daily activities, relationships, and overall well-being. It often involves a pattern of negative thinking that exacerbates feelings of helplessness and panic.

## How Mindfulness Reduces Stress and Anxiety

Mindfulness is the practice of paying attention to the present moment with a non-judgmental attitude. When applied to stress and anxiety, mindfulness helps individuals break the cycle of negative thinking and return to a state of calm.

By focusing on the here and now, mindfulness allows people to step back from their worries and see them from a different perspective.

One of the key ways mindfulness reduces stress and anxiety is by interrupting the automatic response of rumination. Rumination is the tendency to dwell on negative thoughts and worries, which can fuel anxiety and stress. When practicing mindfulness, individuals learn to observe their thoughts without getting caught up in them. This awareness helps to break the cycle of rumination, allowing the mind to rest and recover from the constant barrage of negative thinking.

## Mindfulness Techniques for Managing Stress and Anxiety

There are several mindfulness techniques that can be particularly effective in managing stress and anxiety:

**1. Mindful Breathing:** One of the simplest and most powerful mindfulness practices is mindful breathing. By focusing attention on the breath, individuals can create a calming anchor in the present moment. Mindful breathing helps to regulate the body's stress response by activating the parasympathetic nervous system, which promotes relaxation. It also provides a moment of pause, giving the mind a chance to slow down and release anxious thoughts.

**2. Body Scan Meditation:** The body scan is a mindfulness practice that involves paying attention to physical sensations in different parts of the body. This practice can help individuals become more aware of how stress and anxiety manifest physically, such as through muscle tension or shallow breathing. By bringing awareness to these sensations without trying to change them, the body scan helps to release physical tension and promotes a sense of relaxation.

**3. Mindful Observation:** Mindful observation involves focusing attention on an object or experience in the present moment, such as the sounds in the environment, the sensation of the wind on the skin, or the taste of food. This practice helps to ground individuals in the present moment, reducing the tendency to get lost in worries about the future. By fully engaging the senses, mindful observation can create a sense of calm and peace.

**4.      Loving-Kindness      Meditation:** Loving-kindness meditation is a mindfulness practice that involves directing feelings of compassion and kindness toward oneself and others. This practice can be particularly helpful for those dealing with anxiety, as it helps to counteract negative self-talk and promote feelings of self-acceptance. By cultivating a sense of compassion, loving-kindness meditation can reduce the intensity of anxious thoughts and create a more positive mental state.

## Integrating Mindfulness into Daily Life

One of the strengths of mindfulness is its flexibility—it can be practiced in formal meditation sessions or integrated into daily activities. For those managing stress and anxiety, incorporating mindfulness into everyday routines can be particularly beneficial. Simple practices like taking a few mindful breaths before starting a task, paying full attention to eating a meal, or noticing the sensations in the body while walking can all contribute to a greater sense of calm and presence throughout the day.

Moreover, practicing mindfulness consistently over time can lead to lasting changes in how individuals respond to stress and anxiety. As mindfulness becomes a regular part of life, individuals may find that they are less reactive to stressors, better able to cope with challenges, and more resilient in the face of anxiety.

# CHAPTER 5

# ENHANCING EMOTIONAL WELL-BEING

Emotional well-being is a fundamental aspect of overall health, influencing how we think, feel, and interact with the world around us. It encompasses our ability to manage emotions, cope with stress, build positive relationships, and maintain a sense of purpose and fulfillment in life. While many factors contribute to emotional well-being, mindfulness plays a pivotal role in fostering emotional resilience and balance. By cultivating mindfulness, individuals can enhance their emotional well-being, leading to a richer, more satisfying life.

# Understanding Emotional Well-Being

Emotional well-being is not simply the absence of negative emotions; rather, it is the presence of positive emotions and the ability to navigate life's ups and downs with grace and composure. People with high emotional well-being tend to experience more joy, contentment, and gratitude, while also possessing the tools to manage challenges such as stress, anxiety, and sadness. They are more likely to maintain healthy relationships, achieve personal goals, and experience a sense of purpose in life.

However, emotional well-being is not static. It can fluctuate based on various internal and external factors, such as life events, relationships, and even daily habits. Therefore, it is essential to actively cultivate practices that support and enhance emotional well-being. Mindfulness is one such practice, offering a way to develop greater emotional awareness, resilience, and balance.

## The Role of Mindfulness in Emotional Well-Being

Mindfulness enhances emotional well-being by encouraging a deeper awareness of our thoughts, feelings, and bodily sensations. This heightened awareness allows us to recognize and understand our emotions as they arise, rather than reacting to them impulsively. Through mindfulness, we learn to observe our emotional experiences without judgment, creating space between our emotions and our responses. This practice helps us to manage our emotions more effectively, reducing the intensity of negative emotions and increasing our capacity for positive ones.

One of the key ways mindfulness enhances emotional well-being is by promoting emotional regulation. Emotional regulation is the ability to manage and respond to emotions in a healthy way, rather than being overwhelmed by them. For example, when faced with a stressful situation, a mindful person might notice their rising anxiety and choose to take a few deep breaths, bringing themselves back to a state of calm before responding. This ability to regulate emotions is crucial for maintaining emotional balance and preventing the escalation of negative emotions.

Mindfulness also fosters emotional resilience, which is the capacity to bounce back from difficult emotions or adverse experiences. Emotional resilience does not mean avoiding negative emotions; rather, it involves acknowledging and accepting them without being consumed by them. Through mindfulness, we develop the skills to process and move through challenging emotions, allowing us to recover more quickly and maintain a sense of well-being even in the face of adversity.

## Techniques for Enhancing Emotional Well-Being Through Mindfulness

There are several mindfulness techniques that can be particularly effective in enhancing emotional well-being. These practices help to cultivate emotional awareness, foster self-compassion, and build resilience.

## 1. Mindful Self-Compassion

Mindful self-compassion involves treating yourself with the same kindness and understanding that you would offer to a close friend. Many people are their own harshest critics, engaging in negative self-talk that can erode emotional well-being. Mindful self-compassion encourages a shift in this inner dialogue, replacing self-criticism with self-kindness.

To practice mindful self-compassion, begin by recognizing when you are being hard on yourself. Notice the thoughts and feelings that arise when you make a mistake or fall short of your expectations. Instead of criticizing yourself, try offering words of comfort and encouragement. For example, you might say to yourself, "It's okay to feel this way. Everyone makes mistakes, and I'm doing the best I can."

Mindful self-compassion helps to reduce feelings of shame and inadequacy, fostering a greater sense of emotional well-being. It also creates a foundation of self-acceptance, which is essential for navigating life's challenges with resilience and grace.

**2. Mindful Emotion Awareness**

Mindful emotion awareness involves paying attention to your emotions as they arise, without trying to change or suppress them. This practice encourages you to observe your emotions with curiosity and openness, allowing you to understand them more fully.

To practice mindful emotion awareness, start by taking a few deep breaths to center yourself. Then, bring your attention to the emotions you are experiencing in the present moment. Notice where you feel these emotions in your body—perhaps a tightness in your chest, a knot in your stomach, or warmth in your face. Label the emotion you are feeling, such as "anger," "sadness," or "joy." As you observe your emotions, try to maintain a non-judgmental attitude, simply acknowledging them as they are.

This practice helps to create a sense of distance between you and your emotions, making it easier to respond to them thoughtfully rather than reacting impulsively. By regularly practicing mindful emotion awareness, you can develop a deeper understanding of your emotional landscape, leading to greater emotional intelligence and well-being.

### 3. Gratitude Practice

Gratitude is a powerful emotion that has been shown to enhance emotional well-being. Practicing gratitude involves intentionally focusing on the positive aspects of your life and acknowledging the good things that you often take for granted. This practice can shift your focus from what is lacking to what is abundant, fostering a sense of contentment and joy.

To incorporate gratitude into your mindfulness practice, try keeping a gratitude journal. Each day, write down three things you are grateful for, no matter how small or mundane they may seem. As you write, take a moment to truly feel the gratitude for these things, letting the positive emotions fill your heart and mind.

Gratitude practice can help to counterbalance negative emotions, reducing feelings of anxiety and depression. It also encourages a positive mindset, which is essential for maintaining emotional well-being over the long term.

## 4. Loving-Kindness Meditation

Loving-kindness meditation is a mindfulness practice that involves directing feelings of love and compassion toward yourself and others. This practice helps to cultivate positive emotions such as empathy, compassion, and forgiveness, which are essential for emotional well-being.

To practice loving-kindness meditation, begin by finding a comfortable seated position. Close your eyes and take a few deep breaths. Then, silently repeat phrases of loving-kindness to yourself, such as "May I be happy. May I be healthy. May I be safe. May I live with ease." As you repeat these phrases, try to generate genuine feelings of warmth and kindness toward yourself.

After a few minutes, expand your focus to include others. Start with someone you care about, then gradually extend your loving-kindness to acquaintances, strangers, and even people you find difficult. This practice helps to dissolve feelings of anger and resentment, replacing them with compassion and understanding. By regularly practicing loving-kindness meditation, you can enhance your emotional well-being by cultivating a more positive and empathetic outlook on life.

## The Long-Term Benefits of Mindfulness for Emotional Well-Being

While mindfulness offers immediate benefits for emotional well-being, the long-term effects can be even more profound. Regular mindfulness practice can lead to lasting changes in the brain, increasing areas associated with emotional regulation, empathy, and resilience. Over time, these changes can result in a more stable and balanced emotional state, reducing the frequency and intensity of negative emotions and increasing overall happiness.

Moreover, mindfulness can enhance emotional well-being by improving relationships. As individuals become more aware of their own emotions and more skilled at managing them, they are better equipped to navigate interpersonal conflicts and communicate effectively with others. This can lead to stronger, more fulfilling relationships, which are a key component of emotional well-being.

Finally, mindfulness helps to cultivate a sense of purpose and meaning in life. By encouraging individuals to live fully in the present moment, mindfulness allows them to connect more deeply with their values, passions, and goals. This sense of purpose is essential for emotional well-being, providing a source of motivation and fulfillment that sustains them through life's challenges.

## Developing Healthy Relationships through Mindfulness

Healthy relationships are the cornerstone of a fulfilling life. Whether it's with family, friends, or romantic partners, the quality of our relationships profoundly affects our emotional well-being, self-esteem, and overall happiness. However, relationships also come with challenges, such as miscommunication, unmet expectations, and conflicts, which can strain even the strongest bonds. Mindfulness offers a powerful approach to developing and maintaining healthy relationships by fostering qualities like presence, empathy, patience, and non-judgmental awareness. By integrating mindfulness into our interactions, we can create deeper, more meaningful connections with others.

## The Role of Mindfulness in Relationships

Mindfulness in relationships begins with being fully present in each interaction. This means giving the other person your undivided attention, listening actively, and engaging with them without distractions. In today's world, where multitasking and digital communication often dominate, the simple act of being fully present can be a transformative gesture. When we are present, we signal to others that we value and respect them, which can strengthen trust and intimacy.

Moreover, mindfulness helps us to become more aware of our thoughts, emotions, and reactions in the context of relationships. Often, conflicts arise because we are not fully conscious of the assumptions or judgments we bring into our interactions. For example, we might react defensively to a partner's comment, not because of what they said, but because it triggered an unresolved issue within ourselves. By practicing mindfulness, we can catch these automatic reactions before they escalate, allowing us to respond more thoughtfully and constructively.

## Cultivating Empathy and Compassion

Empathy and compassion are crucial components of healthy relationships. Empathy involves the ability to understand and share the feelings of another person, while compassion goes a step further by motivating us to act in ways that support and care for others. Mindfulness enhances these qualities by encouraging us to approach others with an open heart and a non-judgmental mind.

When we practice mindfulness, we become more attuned to the emotional states of others. We can pick up on subtle cues, such as changes in tone of voice or body language, that might indicate how someone is feeling. This heightened awareness allows us to respond with empathy, validating their emotions and offering support. For instance, if a friend seems upset but isn't expressing it directly, a mindful approach might involve gently asking how they're feeling or simply being present with them in their discomfort.

Compassion in relationships is also fostered by mindfulness. Instead of reacting with frustration or impatience when someone is struggling, mindfulness teaches us to approach them with kindness and understanding. This compassionate stance helps to build a safe and supportive environment where both parties feel valued and cared for. Over time, this can deepen the bond between individuals, creating a relationship that is resilient to the inevitable challenges that arise.

## Mindful Communication

Effective communication is the foundation of any healthy relationship. Mindfulness enhances communication by helping us to be more aware of how we express ourselves and how we listen to others. This includes being mindful of our words, tone, and body language, as well as our intentions behind what we say.

Mindful communication begins with active listening, which involves fully concentrating on what the other person is saying without planning your response or interrupting. This kind of listening shows respect and attentiveness, making the speaker feel heard and understood. It also allows us to grasp the deeper meaning behind the words, which can lead to more meaningful and productive conversations.

In addition to listening, mindfulness also helps us to communicate more clearly and honestly. When we are mindful, we can express our thoughts and feelings without resorting to blame, criticism, or defensiveness. This creates an open and non-threatening environment where both parties feel safe to share their perspectives. For example, instead of saying, "You never listen to me," a more mindful approach might be, "I feel unheard when we talk about certain things, and I would love for us to work on this together."

Another aspect of mindful communication is learning to pause before responding. This pause allows us to check in with ourselves, notice any emotions that might be influencing our response, and choose our words carefully. By taking this moment to reflect, we can avoid reactive or hurtful comments that might damage the relationship. This practice of pausing can be especially valuable during disagreements, where emotions can run high and lead to misunderstandings.

## Handling Conflict with Mindfulness

Conflict is a natural part of any relationship, but how we handle it can determine whether it strengthens or weakens the bond between individuals. Mindfulness provides tools to navigate conflicts in a way that promotes understanding and resolution rather than escalation.

One of the key principles of mindfulness in conflict resolution is non-judgment. When a disagreement arises, it's easy to fall into patterns of blame and judgment, viewing the other person as wrong or at fault. However, mindfulness encourages us to approach the situation with an open mind, considering the perspectives of all parties involved. This doesn't mean that we have to agree with the other person, but it does mean acknowledging their experience without immediately dismissing it.

Mindfulness also helps us to stay present during conflicts, rather than getting lost in past grievances or future worries. By focusing on the present moment, we can address the issue at hand without letting it spiral into a larger argument. This present-focused approach allows us to communicate more clearly, listen more deeply, and work together to find a solution.

Another important aspect of handling conflict mindfully is recognizing our own triggers. These are the specific words, actions, or situations that provoke a strong emotional reaction in us. By becoming aware of our triggers, we can better manage our responses during conflicts. For instance, if we know that we tend to react defensively when criticized, we can use mindfulness to notice this reaction as it arises, take a deep breath, and choose to respond in a more constructive way.

## Strengthening Relationships Through Mindful Practice

Mindfulness is not just a tool for resolving conflicts or improving communication; it's a practice that can continually strengthen relationships over time. By regularly engaging in mindfulness, we develop greater emotional awareness, patience, and compassion—all qualities that contribute to the health and longevity of our relationships.

One way to integrate mindfulness into relationships is through shared practices. This could involve meditating together, practicing mindful listening, or simply setting aside time each day to connect without distractions. These shared practices help to reinforce the bond between individuals, creating a sense of togetherness and mutual support.

Additionally, mindfulness helps us to appreciate the positive aspects of our relationships. In the busyness of everyday life, it's easy to take loved ones for granted or focus on their flaws. Mindfulness encourages us to notice and savor the moments of connection, joy, and love that we experience with others. This practice of gratitude can enhance the overall quality of our relationships, making them more fulfilling and meaningful.

# CHAPTER 6

# MINDFULNESS AND PERSONAL GROWTH

Personal growth is a lifelong journey, encompassing the continuous development of our character, skills, and self-awareness. It involves striving to reach our full potential, pursuing meaningful goals, and becoming the best version of ourselves. However, personal growth is not always a straightforward path; it requires introspection, patience, and a willingness to face challenges and discomfort. Mindfulness offers a powerful tool for fostering personal growth by encouraging us to live with greater awareness, intention, and compassion.

## The Connection Between Mindfulness and Personal Growth

Mindfulness and personal growth are deeply intertwined. At its core, mindfulness is about being fully present in the moment, cultivating an awareness of our thoughts, emotions, and behaviors without judgment. This heightened awareness is essential for personal growth because it allows us to gain a deeper understanding of ourselves, including our strengths, weaknesses, habits, and motivations.

When we practice mindfulness, we become more attuned to our inner experiences, which can illuminate areas of our lives where growth is needed. For example, mindfulness might help us recognize patterns of negative thinking that hold us back or reveal unhelpful habits that we were previously unaware of. By bringing these aspects of ourselves into conscious awareness, we can begin to address them and make meaningful changes.

Moreover, mindfulness encourages a mindset of acceptance and non-judgment, which is crucial for personal growth. Often, we are our own harshest critics, judging ourselves harshly for our perceived shortcomings or mistakes. This self-criticism can create a barrier to growth, making it difficult to move forward. Mindfulness teaches us to approach ourselves with kindness and compassion, recognizing that growth is a process that involves both successes and setbacks. This self-compassionate attitude allows us to embrace our imperfections and view them as opportunities for learning and development.

## Mindfulness as a Tool for Self-Discovery

Personal growth begins with self-discovery—the process of exploring and understanding who we are at our core. Mindfulness facilitates self-discovery by encouraging us to observe our thoughts, emotions, and behaviors with curiosity and openness. Through mindfulness, we can uncover the underlying beliefs and values that drive our actions, as well as the fears and insecurities that may be holding us back.

One of the key aspects of self-discovery through mindfulness is the ability to observe our thoughts without becoming attached to them. In our day-to-day lives, we are often caught up in our thoughts, identifying with them as if they were absolute truths. However, mindfulness teaches us that our thoughts are simply mental events that come and go. By observing our thoughts mindfully, we can gain insight into the patterns and beliefs that shape our behavior, without being controlled by them.

For example, you might notice a recurring thought like "I'm not good enough," which has influenced your actions and decisions. Through mindfulness, you can observe this thought without judgment, recognizing it as a limiting belief rather than a fact. This awareness opens the door to personal growth, allowing you to challenge and reframe these limiting beliefs.

## Setting Intentions for Growth

Another way mindfulness supports personal growth is by helping us to set clear and intentional goals. Personal growth is most effective when it is guided by a sense of purpose and direction. However, it's easy to set goals that are based on external expectations or societal pressures, rather than our true desires and values. Mindfulness helps us to connect with our authentic selves, ensuring that the goals we set are aligned with our deepest values and aspirations.

When setting intentions for growth, mindfulness encourages us to reflect on what truly matters to us. This might involve asking ourselves questions like, "What do I want to contribute to the world?" or "What kind of person do I want to become?" By taking the time to explore these questions mindfully, we can set goals that are meaningful and fulfilling, rather than superficial or externally driven.

In addition to helping us set intentional goals, mindfulness also supports us in pursuing those goals with patience and perseverance. Personal growth is not always a linear process; it often involves setbacks and challenges. Mindfulness teaches us to approach these obstacles with a calm and patient mindset, viewing them as opportunities for learning rather than as failures. This resilience is essential for sustaining personal growth over the long term.

## Overcoming Obstacles to Personal Growth with Mindfulness

The path of personal growth is not without its challenges. As we strive to grow and improve, we may encounter various obstacles, such as fear, self-doubt, procrastination, and resistance to change. These obstacles can hinder our progress if not addressed. Mindfulness provides valuable tools for overcoming these challenges by helping us to recognize and work through them with awareness and compassion.

One common obstacle to personal growth is fear, particularly the fear of failure or the unknown. Fear can paralyze us, preventing us from taking the necessary steps toward growth. Mindfulness helps us to confront our fears by bringing them into conscious awareness and examining them objectively. By observing our fears mindfully, we can begin to understand their origins and see them for what they are—natural responses to uncertainty, rather than insurmountable barriers. This awareness allows us to take action despite our fears, moving forward on our path of growth.

Another challenge that often arises in the pursuit of personal growth is self-doubt. Many of us struggle with feelings of inadequacy or impostor syndrome, which can undermine our confidence and motivation. Mindfulness helps to counteract self-doubt by fostering self-compassion and self-acceptance. Through mindfulness, we learn to recognize and challenge our negative self-talk, replacing it with more supportive and empowering thoughts. This shift in mindset can bolster our confidence, enabling us to pursue our goals with greater determination.

Procrastination is another common obstacle to personal growth. It's easy to put off tasks or goals that feel overwhelming or uncomfortable, delaying our progress. Mindfulness helps us to break the cycle of procrastination by bringing our attention to the present moment and the task at hand. When we practice mindfulness, we can notice the thoughts and emotions that trigger procrastination—such as fear, boredom, or resistance—without giving in to them. This awareness allows us to take action, even when it feels challenging, and to build momentum toward our goals.

Resistance to change is a natural human response, as growth often requires us to step out of our comfort zones and embrace the unfamiliar. Mindfulness helps us to navigate resistance by encouraging us to stay present with the discomfort that comes with change, rather than avoiding it. By sitting with our discomfort mindfully, we can gradually become more comfortable with uncertainty and change, opening ourselves up to new possibilities for growth.

## Integrating Mindfulness into Daily Life for Continuous Growth

To fully harness the power of mindfulness for personal growth, it's important to integrate mindfulness into our daily lives. This means going beyond formal meditation practice and finding ways to bring mindfulness into our everyday activities and interactions.

One way to do this is by practicing mindful awareness throughout the day. This involves paying attention to whatever you are doing, whether it's eating, walking, working, or spending time with loved ones. By bringing your full attention to the present moment, you can deepen your connection with yourself and the world around you, creating a fertile ground for personal growth.

Another way to integrate mindfulness into daily life is by setting aside time for regular reflection. This might involve journaling about your experiences, thoughts, and emotions, or simply taking a few moments each day to sit quietly and observe your inner landscape. Regular reflection allows you to track your progress, identify areas for growth, and celebrate your achievements.

Finally, mindfulness can be integrated into your interactions with others. This might involve practicing mindful listening, where you give your full attention to the person you are speaking with, or expressing gratitude and appreciation for the people in your life. By bringing mindfulness into your relationships, you not only foster personal growth but also create more meaningful and fulfilling connections with others.

# Embracing Change and Uncertainty

Change and uncertainty are inevitable aspects of life. No matter how much we plan or prepare, we are bound to encounter situations that challenge our expectations, disrupt our routines, and push us out of our comfort zones. While these experiences can be unsettling, they also offer significant opportunities for growth and transformation. Mindfulness provides a powerful framework for embracing change and uncertainty with grace, resilience, and an open heart.

## Understanding the Nature of Change

At its core, mindfulness teaches us to accept the impermanent nature of life. Everything around us is in a constant state of flux—our thoughts, emotions, relationships, and circumstances. This understanding can be both liberating and daunting. On one hand, it reminds us that difficult times will eventually pass. On the other, it challenges us to let go of our attachments to the way things are or the way we wish they would be.

Mindfulness helps us navigate change by encouraging us to remain present, even when our surroundings or internal experiences are shifting. Instead of resisting change or trying to control it, mindfulness invites us to observe it with curiosity and openness. This shift in perspective allows us to see change not as a threat, but as an integral part of the journey of life—an opportunity to learn, adapt, and grow.

## Embracing Uncertainty with Mindfulness

Uncertainty often goes hand in hand with change. When we face the unknown, it's natural to feel anxious or fearful. However, these emotions can become overwhelming if we allow them to dominate our thoughts. Mindfulness offers an alternative approach by helping us to stay grounded in the present moment, rather than getting lost in worries about the future.

By practicing mindfulness, we learn to acknowledge our fears without letting them control us. This involves noticing the sensations in our body, the thoughts in our mind, and the emotions that arise in response to uncertainty. Instead of reacting impulsively or trying to avoid discomfort, we can choose to sit with our experience, observing it with a sense of detachment. This mindful awareness creates space between ourselves and our fears, allowing us to respond to uncertainty with calmness and clarity.

Mindfulness also encourages us to embrace uncertainty as a natural part of life. Rather than seeking certainty or predictability in every situation, we can cultivate a mindset of flexibility and openness. This doesn't mean that we give up on planning or preparing for the future, but it does mean that we learn to accept the limitations of our control. By letting go of the need for certainty, we free ourselves from the anxiety that often accompanies it, allowing us to approach life's challenges with a greater sense of ease.

## The Growth that Comes from Embracing Change

Embracing change and uncertainty through mindfulness is not just about coping with difficult situations; it's about recognizing the potential for growth that lies within them. When we allow ourselves to be fully present with change, we open the door to new experiences, perspectives, and possibilities. We become more adaptable, resilient, and open-minded—qualities that are essential for personal growth.

Moreover, by embracing change, we learn to trust in our ability to navigate life's ups and downs. Each time we face a challenge with mindfulness, we build our confidence and inner strength. We come to see that we are capable of handling whatever life throws our way, not by resisting or avoiding it, but by meeting it with presence, acceptance, and curiosity.

# Achieving Balance and Fulfillment

Achieving balance and fulfillment in life is a dynamic process that requires ongoing attention and mindful intention. In a world where demands and distractions are constant, finding a sense of equilibrium can feel challenging. Yet, mindfulness offers a pathway to this balance by encouraging us to stay connected to our values, prioritize what truly matters, and engage fully in each aspect of our lives.

## The Role of Mindfulness in Finding Balance

Mindfulness helps us to recognize when our lives are out of balance. By paying attention to our thoughts, emotions, and physical sensations, we can identify the areas where we are overextended or neglecting our needs. This awareness allows us to make conscious choices that align with our values and goals, whether it's setting boundaries, adjusting our schedules, or taking time for self-care.

## Cultivating Fulfillment Through Presence

Fulfillment is deeply connected to our ability to be present in the moment. When we practice mindfulness, we engage more fully in our activities, whether they are related to work, relationships, or personal interests. This presence enhances our sense of purpose and satisfaction, as we are able to experience life more deeply and authentically.

# CHAPTER 7

# INTEGRATING MINDFULNESS INTO DAILY LIFE

Integrating mindfulness into daily life is about making a conscious choice to bring awareness, presence, and intentionality into every aspect of your day. While formal mindfulness practices like meditation or yoga provide foundational tools for cultivating mindfulness, the real transformation occurs when you extend this awareness beyond the practice space and into your everyday experiences. This chapter explores how you can seamlessly weave mindfulness into your daily routines, interactions, and activities, thereby enriching your life with greater clarity, calmness, and contentment.

## Mindful Mornings: Starting the Day with Presence

The way you begin your day sets the tone for the hours that follow. Starting your morning with mindfulness can help you approach the day with a calm, clear, and focused mindset. Rather than rushing through your morning routine or immediately diving into tasks, consider creating a mindful morning ritual.

Begin with several minutes of deep breathing or a brief meditation. This simple practice can help you center yourself, bringing your awareness to the present moment and setting a positive intention for the day. Even if your morning is busy, taking just a moment to breathe mindfully can make a significant difference.

As you continue with your morning activities—whether it's brushing your teeth, making breakfast, or getting dressed—try to remain fully present. Pay attention to the sensations, smells, sounds, and movements involved in each task. For example, notice the feel of the water as you wash your face, the texture of your clothing as you put it on, or the taste of your first sip of coffee. These moments of mindfulness help ground you in the present and foster a sense of calm as you start your day.

## Mindful Eating: Nourishing Body and Mind

Eating is an activity that most of us engage in several times a day, yet it's often done on autopilot. Mindful eating is about bringing full awareness to the experience of eating—savoring each bite, noticing the flavors, textures, and smells, and paying attention to the body's hunger and satiety signals.

To practice mindful eating, start by taking a moment to appreciate your food before you begin eating. Observe its colors, shapes, and aromas. As you take each bite, chew slowly and notice the flavors and textures as they unfold. Pay attention to how your body feels as you eat, and try to eat without distractions like television, smartphones, or other screens.

Mindful eating not only improves your enjoyment of meals but also promotes healthy eating habits. By tuning in to your body's cues, you're more likely to eat when you're hungry, stop when you're full, and choose foods that truly nourish you. This mindful approach to eating can also help you develop a healthier relationship with food, reducing overeating and emotional eating.

## Mindful Movement: Bringing Awareness to Physical Activity

Physical activity is another area where mindfulness can be easily integrated. Whether you're engaging in formal exercise, stretching, walking, or simply moving throughout your day, mindful movement involves paying attention to the sensations in your body as you move.

For example, during a walk, you can practice mindfulness by noticing the feeling of your feet as they make contact with the ground, the rhythm of your breath, and the sights and sounds around you. If you're exercising, focus on the sensations of your muscles working, the flow of your breath, and the way your body moves through space.

Mindful movement helps you connect with your body, enhancing the physical and mental benefits of exercise. It also encourages you to listen to your body's needs, whether that means pushing yourself a little further or recognizing when to rest. This practice can turn any form of movement into a meditative experience, promoting both physical health and mental well-being.

## Mindful Working: Bringing Focus and Clarity to Your Tasks

For many people, work is a significant part of daily life, and it's easy to become overwhelmed by the demands and distractions that come with it. Mindfulness can help you approach your work with greater focus, efficiency, and satisfaction by bringing your full attention to the task at hand.

One way to practice mindfulness at work is by starting each task with a moment of intentional focus. Before diving into a new task, take a deep breath, and set a clear intention for what you want to accomplish. Throughout the task, try to remain fully engaged, noticing when your mind starts to wander and gently bringing your attention back to the present moment.

Taking short mindfulness breaks during the workday can also help you maintain clarity and prevent burnout. Even just a few minutes of mindful breathing or stretching can refresh your mind and body, allowing you to return to your work with renewed focus.

Additionally, practicing mindful communication at work—listening fully to others without interrupting, responding thoughtfully rather than reacting impulsively, and being aware of your tone and body language—can improve your relationships with coworkers and foster a more friendly workplace atmosphere.

## Mindful Interactions: Deepening Connections with Others

Mindfulness can transform the way you interact with others by helping you to be fully present in your relationships. Whether you're having a conversation with a friend, spending time with family, or engaging with colleagues, mindful interactions involve giving your full attention to the person in front of you.

One way to practice mindful communication is by listening deeply. This means listening not only to the words being spoken but also to the emotions and intentions behind them. It involves being fully present, without thinking about what you'll say next or letting your mind wander to other things.

When you respond, do so mindfully. Take a moment to consider your words and how they might be received. Mindful communication encourages empathy, understanding, and more meaningful connections, helping to nurture healthier and more fulfilling relationships.

## Mindful Evenings: Unwinding and Reflecting

Just as the way you start your day can set the tone for what follows, the way you end your day can impact your sleep and overall well-being. Incorporating mindfulness into your nightly routine can help you relax, let go of the day's stresses, and prepare for a good night's sleep.

Consider establishing an evening mindfulness practice, such as a short meditation, mindful stretching, or journaling about your day. Reflecting on your experiences, acknowledging what you're grateful for, and setting an intention for the following day can help you transition smoothly from the busyness of the day to a state of relaxation.

Mindful breathing exercises before bed can also help calm your mind and body, making it easier to fall asleep. Focus on your breath, noticing the rise and fall of your chest, the sensation of air entering and leaving your nostrils, and the way your body feels as it begins to relax.

## Embracing Mindfulness in Everyday Activities

Integrating mindfulness into daily life isn't limited to specific practices or routines; it's about bringing a mindful attitude to all of your activities. Whether you're cooking, cleaning, driving, or engaging in a hobby, mindfulness can transform even the most mundane tasks into opportunities for presence and reflection.

For example, while washing dishes, instead of rushing through the task, focus on the sensation of the warm water, the feel of the soap, and the sound of the dishes clinking together. When you're driving, notice the feel of the steering wheel in your hands, the sights and sounds around you, and the rhythm of your breath.

These moments of mindfulness throughout your day can help you stay grounded, reduce stress, and enhance your overall sense of well-being. By approaching each task with full awareness, you cultivate a deeper connection to the present moment and a greater appreciation for the simple things in life.

## Using Mindfulness for Problem-Solving and Decision-Making

Mindfulness, often associated with reducing stress and increasing well-being, also plays a pivotal role in enhancing problem-solving and decision-making skills. When faced with complex challenges or important decisions, the clarity and presence that mindfulness fosters can lead to more thoughtful, effective outcomes.

## Cultivating Clarity and Focus

One of the primary ways mindfulness aids in problem-solving is by sharpening focus and clarity. When your mind is cluttered with distractions or emotions, it's difficult to see a situation clearly. Mindfulness helps you to clear mental noise by bringing your attention to the present moment. Through practices like mindful breathing or a short meditation, you can calm your mind and create space for clearer thinking. This mental clarity allows you to approach problems with a fresh perspective, enabling you to see details and connections that might otherwise go unnoticed.

## Enhancing Emotional Regulation

Decision-making is often influenced by emotions, which can cloud judgment and lead to impulsive choices. Mindfulness teaches emotional awareness and regulation, helping you to recognize and acknowledge your feelings without being overwhelmed by them. When emotions arise during problem-solving or decision-making, a mindful approach allows you to pause, observe the emotion, and let it pass before taking action. This detachment from immediate emotional reactions leads to more balanced, reasoned decisions that are less influenced by stress, fear, or frustration.

## Encouraging Open-Mindedness

Mindfulness encourages an open-minded approach to problem-solving by promoting curiosity and non-judgment. When you're mindful, you're more likely to explore all possibilities rather than jumping to conclusions. This openness allows you to consider a wider range of solutions and perspectives, leading to more innovative and effective problem-solving. Moreover, mindfulness helps to reduce cognitive biases, such as confirmation bias, by encouraging you to remain open to new information and different viewpoints.

## Facilitating Reflective Decision-Making

Mindfulness fosters a reflective decision-making process. Instead of making decisions hastily, mindfulness encourages taking a step back to reflect on all aspects of a situation. This reflection includes considering the potential outcomes, weighing the pros and cons, and aligning the decision with your values and goals. By integrating mindfulness into decision-making, you make choices that are not only more informed but also more in tune with your long-term objectives and well-being.

# CHAPTER 8

# ADVANCED MINDFULNESS PRACTICES

As your mindfulness journey deepens, you may find yourself ready to explore more advanced practices that build upon the foundational techniques of mindfulness. These advanced practices are designed to enhance your awareness, cultivate deeper states of concentration, and facilitate profound personal growth. This chapter delves into some of these advanced mindfulness practices, offering guidance on how to incorporate them into your life and experience their transformative effects.

## Deepening Your Practice with Extended Meditation Sessions

One of the key elements of advanced mindfulness is the practice of extended meditation sessions. While shorter, daily meditations are essential for maintaining a regular mindfulness practice, longer sessions—ranging from 30 minutes to an hour or more—allow you to delve deeper into the mind and explore states of awareness that are difficult to access in shorter periods.

During extended meditation, you have the opportunity to observe the mind's activity over an extended period, noticing patterns and tendencies that may not be apparent in brief sessions. This practice encourages a deeper sense of stillness and concentration, enabling you to move beyond surface-level thoughts and emotions. As you continue to sit in meditation, you may experience moments of profound clarity, insight, or a sense of unity with the present moment.

To incorporate extended meditation sessions into your routine, start by gradually increasing the duration of your daily meditation. For example, if you typically meditate for 15 minutes, try extending your sessions to 20 or 30 minutes. Over time, you can work up to longer sessions, allowing your mind and body to adapt to the practice. Remember that the goal is not to force longer meditations but to approach them with curiosity and openness, allowing the practice to unfold naturally.

## Exploring Insight Meditation (Vipassana)

Insight meditation, also known as Vipassana, is a traditional Buddhist practice that focuses on developing deep awareness and understanding of the nature of reality. Unlike concentration-based meditation practices that focus on a single point of attention, Vipassana encourages the practitioner to observe the arising and passing of sensations, thoughts, and emotions in a non-reactive and non-judgmental way.

The primary aim of Vipassana is to gain insight into the impermanent and interconnected nature of all experiences. By observing the impermanence of thoughts and sensations, practitioners develop a greater understanding of the transient nature of life and the concept of non-self—the realization that the self is not a fixed, unchanging entity but a collection of constantly changing processes.

To practice Vipassana, start by sitting in a comfortable position and bringing your attention to your breath. As you become more aware of your breath, begin to expand your awareness to include bodily sensations, emotions, and thoughts. Observe these experiences without trying to change them, simply noting their presence and observing how they arise, persist, and eventually pass away.

Through regular practice, Vipassana can lead to profound insights into the nature of suffering, attachment, and the true nature of reality. These insights can have a transformative effect on your life, leading to greater inner peace, compassion, and a deeper understanding of yourself and the world around you.

## Cultivating Loving-Kindness (Metta) Meditation

Loving-kindness meditation, or Metta, is an advanced mindfulness practice that focuses on cultivating feelings of compassion, love, and kindness towards oneself and others. This practice involves generating positive, loving thoughts and directing them towards yourself, loved ones, acquaintances, strangers, and even those with whom you have difficult relationships.

To practice Metta, begin by sitting comfortably and bringing your attention to your heart center. Start by generating feelings of warmth and love towards yourself, silently repeating phrases such as "May I be happy, may I be healthy, may I be safe, may I live with ease." Once you've formed these feelings of loving-kindness for yourself, gradually extend them to others, beginning with someone you care about, then progressing to a neutral person, and lastly to someone with whom you disagree.

The practice of Metta can be deeply transformative, helping to soften the heart, reduce feelings of anger or resentment, and foster a greater sense of connection with others. Over time, this practice can lead to increased emotional resilience, compassion, and a more profound sense of interconnectedness with all beings.

## Engaging in Mindful Inquiry and Reflection

Mindful inquiry and reflection are advanced practices that involve exploring the deeper layers of your thoughts, beliefs, and emotions with a sense of curiosity and openness. These practices are often used to investigate specific challenges, patterns, or questions that arise during meditation or daily life.

To engage in mindful inquiry, begin by identifying a particular issue or question you wish to explore. This could be a recurring thought pattern, an emotional response, or a life situation that you find challenging. Once you have identified your focus, bring it into your awareness during meditation, observing it with curiosity and without judgment.

Consider asking yourself open-ended questions like, "What is this experience teaching me?" or "How does this feeling arise in my body?" Allow yourself to sit with the question, observing any thoughts, sensations, or emotions that arise without trying to force an answer. The goal is not to find a solution but to deepen your understanding of the experience.

Mindful reflection can also be practiced outside of formal meditation, through journaling or quiet contemplation. By regularly engaging in mindful inquiry, you can gain valuable insights into your inner world, identify patterns that may be holding you back, and develop a more profound understanding of yourself and your life.

## Practicing Mindfulness in Silence and Solitude

Silence and solitude are powerful tools for deepening your mindfulness practice. Spending time in silence, whether through a silent retreat or by incorporating periods of silence into your daily life, allows you to turn inward and connect more deeply with your inner experiences.

During periods of silence, you may notice an increased awareness of your thoughts, emotions, and physical sensations. Without the usual distractions of conversation, media, or external stimuli, you have the opportunity to observe the subtle workings of your mind more clearly. This heightened awareness can lead to profound insights, greater emotional clarity, and a deeper sense of inner peace.

If you're interested in exploring mindfulness in silence, consider attending a silent retreat, where you can immerse yourself in meditation and mindful living without the distractions of daily life. Alternatively, you can create your own mini-retreat at home by setting aside a day or weekend for silence, during which you refrain from speaking, using technology, or engaging in other distractions.

## Applying Mindfulness to Complex Life Challenges

As your mindfulness practice deepens, you can begin to apply mindfulness to more complex life challenges, such as navigating major life transitions, dealing with difficult emotions, or addressing long-standing patterns of behavior. Advanced mindfulness practices can help you approach these challenges with greater clarity, resilience, and compassion.

For example, when facing a significant life transition, such as a career change or the loss of a loved one, mindfulness can help you stay present with the emotions and uncertainties that arise. By bringing mindful awareness to your thoughts and feelings, you can avoid becoming overwhelmed by the situation and instead respond with greater wisdom and calm.

Similarly, when dealing with difficult emotions, such as anger, fear, or sadness, advanced mindfulness practices can help you explore these emotions more deeply, uncovering their underlying causes and learning how to respond to them in a healthy, constructive way.

## Deepening Your Mindfulness Practice

As you progress in your mindfulness journey, the desire to deepen your practice naturally emerges. Deepening mindfulness involves not only refining existing techniques but also exploring new dimensions of awareness that can further enrich your experience. This progression is about cultivating a more profound connection with the present moment and integrating mindfulness more fully into your daily life.

## Consistency and Intention

One of the most effective ways to deepen your mindfulness practice is through consistency and intention. Establishing a regular practice, even if it's just a few minutes each day, creates a strong foundation for growth. The key is to approach each session with clear intention—whether it's to explore a specific aspect of your experience, cultivate a particular quality like compassion or patience, or simply to observe your breath. By infusing your practice with intention, you bring more focus and depth to each moment.

## Exploring Different Techniques

Another way to deepen your mindfulness practice is by exploring different meditation techniques. While you may have started with basic breath awareness or body scan practices, experimenting with other forms of meditation can open new pathways to mindfulness. Techniques like loving-kindness meditation, also known as Metta, or walking meditation, where you focus on the sensations of movement, offer diverse approaches to cultivating mindfulness. Each technique highlights different aspects of awareness, allowing you to deepen your understanding and experience.

## Integrating Mindfulness into Everyday Activities

Mindfulness isn't confined to formal meditation sessions; it's a practice that can be woven into every aspect of your life. Deepening your mindfulness practice involves bringing mindful awareness to routine activities such as eating, walking, or even washing dishes. By fully engaging with these activities and paying attention to the sensations, thoughts, and emotions that arise, you transform mundane moments into opportunities for mindfulness. This integration of mindfulness into daily life fosters a continuous state of awareness, making it easier to remain present throughout the day.

## Embracing Challenges

As you deepen your mindfulness practice, you'll likely encounter challenges such as restlessness, boredom, or difficult emotions. Rather than seeing these challenges as obstacles, view them as opportunities to deepen your practice. Each challenge presents a chance to observe your mind's habitual patterns and to cultivate greater resilience and acceptance. By embracing these difficulties with curiosity and compassion, you can move beyond superficial mindfulness into a deeper, more transformative practice.

## Finding Advanced Resources and Communities

As your mindfulness practice deepens, you may seek advanced resources and communities to further support your growth. Engaging with these resources can offer new perspectives, techniques, and connections that enrich your journey and help you overcome challenges.

## Exploring Advanced Resources

There are many advanced resources available for those looking to deepen their mindfulness practice. Books and courses by experienced mindfulness teachers provide in-depth explorations of specific techniques, philosophies, and applications of mindfulness. Titles by renowned authors like Jon Kabat-Zinn, Pema Chödrön, and Thich Nhat Hanh offer insights into advanced practices, such as insight meditation, loving-kindness, and mindful living. Additionally, online platforms like Insight Timer and Headspace offer guided meditations tailored for experienced practitioners, along with workshops and talks that dive into complex aspects of mindfulness.

## Joining Mindfulness Communities

Connecting with a community of like-minded individuals can greatly enhance your mindfulness practice. Joining a local meditation group or attending a retreat allows you to practice with others, share experiences, and receive guidance from seasoned practitioners. These communities often provide a supportive environment where you can discuss challenges, gain new insights, and stay motivated.

Online communities also offer valuable support, especially for those who may not have access to local groups. Forums, social media groups, and virtual meditation sessions connect you with practitioners worldwide, fostering a sense of belonging and shared purpose. These platforms often feature discussions on advanced topics, book recommendations, and live teachings from mindfulness experts.

# CONCLUSION

As we reach the end of this journey through "Nurturing the Present: Unlocking the Power of Mindfulness to Transform Your Life and Well-Being," it's time to reflect on the key insights and practices that have been explored. This book has taken you through the essence of mindfulness, the importance of living in the present moment, and the practical steps you can take to integrate mindfulness into every aspect of your life. By revisiting these themes, you can solidify your understanding and ensure that the transformative power of mindfulness continues to shape your life for the better.

## Embracing the Present Moment

The foundation of mindfulness lies in the ability to fully embrace the present moment. Throughout this book, we've emphasized the significance of being present, recognizing that the here and now is the only moment we truly have. By learning to focus on the present, you can reduce the mental clutter of past regrets and future anxieties, creating a space for peace and clarity. Whether through simple breath awareness, body scans, or mindful observation, the practices outlined here are designed to anchor you in the present, allowing you to experience life more fully and authentically.

## Overcoming Barriers and Developing a Mindfulness Practice

As with any journey, the path to mindfulness is not without its obstacles. Common barriers like distractions, emotional turbulence, and habitual thinking patterns can make it challenging to stay present. However, by recognizing these barriers and employing the strategies discussed—such as setting clear intentions, practicing patience, and approaching challenges with curiosity—you can overcome them and deepen your mindfulness practice. Developing a consistent mindfulness practice, whether through daily meditation, mindful movement, or integrating mindfulness into everyday activities, is essential for fostering lasting change.

## Enhancing Emotional Well-Being and Relationships

Mindfulness has a profound impact on emotional well-being, offering tools to manage stress, anxiety, and difficult emotions. By cultivating awareness and compassion through practices like loving-kindness meditation and mindful inquiry, you can develop greater emotional resilience and a more balanced perspective on life's challenges. Furthermore, mindfulness enhances your relationships by fostering empathy, active listening, and emotional regulation. As you become more mindful in your interactions, you can build stronger, healthier connections with others, creating a ripple effect of positivity in your personal and professional life.

## Supporting Personal Growth and Navigating Change

Mindfulness is also a powerful catalyst for personal growth. By bringing mindful awareness to your thoughts, behaviors, and life circumstances, you can identify areas for growth and transformation. This book has highlighted how mindfulness supports you in embracing change and uncertainty, helping you navigate life's transitions with grace and confidence. Whether facing a major life decision, adapting to new circumstances, or simply striving to live more authentically, mindfulness provides the clarity and inner strength needed to move forward with purpose.

## Integrating Mindfulness into Daily Life

The ultimate goal of mindfulness is to weave it into the fabric of your daily life, making it a natural part of who you are and how you engage with the world. The practices and techniques discussed in this book—ranging from mindful breathing to advanced meditation and reflective inquiry—are all tools to help you achieve this integration. By consistently applying these practices, you can maintain a state of mindful awareness throughout your day, allowing you to respond to life's challenges with wisdom, compassion, and equanimity.

## Moving Forward with Mindfulness

As you continue on your mindfulness journey, remember that this is an ongoing process of growth and discovery. The principles and practices you've learned in this book are just the beginning. Whether you're deepening your practice through advanced techniques, exploring new resources and communities, or simply refining your ability to stay present, there is always more to learn and experience.

Mindfulness is not about reaching a final destination but about continuously nurturing the present moment, cultivating awareness, and embracing life as it unfolds. By committing to this practice, you can transform your life, enhance your well-being, and create a more mindful, fulfilled existence.